From the Front Lines to the Sidelines

Field-Proven Leadership for Fathers,
Coaches, and Warrior Mentors.
Justin Sedelmaier

This book is available in quantity at discount for yourgroup or organization. For further information, contact:

The Warrior Coach

9323 Northwood Hwy

Onekama, MI 49675

760-927-5740

contact@the-warrior-coach.com

Printed in the United States of America

ISBN 979-8-218-75053-4

Contents

Dedication Page

To my wife Amber-

Your strength, sacrifice, and unwavering belief in me have been the foundation of every mission I've taken on. You held the line through deployments, long nights, and uncertain seasons. This book wouldn't exist without your love and support.

To my children Jason, Hazel, and Remington-

You are my legacy. Everything I teach on the field, I try to live at home. I hope this book helps you understand what leadership, love, and purpose really look like. Lead boldly, love fiercely, and never forget that your father believes in you, always.

Acknowledgments

To try and give credit in this book for each idea, phrase, and concept that I have picked up from other sources along my journey would be impossible. As coaches and leaders we are a combination of the collective experiences of those we have worked with and learned from. I have learned something from nearly every coach I have ever came into contact with and would never submit that the ideas and principles in this book as original. Instead, they are a collection of concepts and observations that I have personally used to shape the teams I have had the honor to be a part of. I hope that each one of you who read this are able to use these same ideas and guiding principles to better the lives of those around you by making it your own.

-J.S.

Prologue

The Call

Leaving the Marine Corps was one of the hardest transitions of my life. Not because I missed the uniform, but because I lost the mission.

In the Corps, I knew exactly who I was. I had purpose. I had direction. I had a brotherhood that would go through hell with me. I never had to wonder if I was making a difference; I saw it in the men around me, in the work we did, in the unity we forged.

But when I got out, all of that disappeared.

I couldn't relate to civilians. I found their attitude and work ethic hard to stomach. They complained about things I used to dream of having, like air conditioning, regular hours, or a boss who didn't yell.

Finding a job was another battle. I had been the assistant operations chief of an infantry battalion, but most employers saw nothing but a blank piece of paper. I didn't have a degree. I didn't have the right "credentials."

It crushed me.

I felt like a failure. Like all the blood, sweat, and leadership I had poured into the Corps meant nothing. I fell into depression. Isolated myself. Got angry. There were days I didn't want to talk to anyone. Days I questioned whether my best years were behind me.

And then: football.

I went to watch a game at my old high school and had a conversation about football with an assistant coach afterward. Later, my former coach invited me to come help. Just volunteer. Just be around the players.

I was hesitant, but I loved football. I loved mentoring. And deep down, I was desperate for purpose.

So, I showed up.

And it changed everything.

Suddenly, I had young men looking up to me. Listening. Asking questions. Craving discipline. Needing strength. I wasn't just drawing plays on a whiteboard. I was giving them things I'd nearly lost: structure, accountability, and belief.

And they gave it back to me.

Coaching didn't just fill the gap after the military, it reignited my mission.

This book isn't a strategy manual. It's a mission brief.

If you're holding these pages, there's a reason.

Maybe you've been through hell. Maybe you've seen what happens when young men drift without standards, without discipline, without direction.

Maybe you're tired of watching society sideline real strength. Maybe you've been searching for something more.

This book is your call to arms.

Because we don't just need more coaches. We need more men who lead like warriors.

The battlefield has changed. But the mission hasn't.

What follows is your path from the fire to the front lines. From the locker room to the living room. From influence to impact.

You are being called to lead. Let's get to work.

Introduction

The Warrior Coach Mission

I didn't plan on becoming a coach.

After my time in the Marine Corps, I was invited to help as an assistant at my old high school. Nothing serious. But the moment I stepped onto that field, everything changed. I didn't just see football players, I saw young Marines. Teenagers on the edge of manhood. Some cocky, some quiet, most carrying heavy burdens.

They needed more than a coach—they needed someone who had walked through fire and come out stronger.

One moment sealed it.

During practice, a player and coach got into a heated argument. I stepped in and pulled the player aside.

"I won't allow a player to disrespect a coach—no matter the reason," I said.

He looked me in the eye and admitted his home life was falling apart. His dad was either at work or at the bar, leaving him to raise his younger brother.

I gave him my number and told him to call anytime. He hugged me. That began a two-year mentorship that changed his life. He grew into a disciplined, dependable young man.

Another time, a quiet player lingered after practice. I asked how he was. That small gesture led to a conversation about his fears and pressures at home. Over the following weeks, I invested in him. He became a solid, respected player. He later said that moment changed how he viewed himself.

Both young men overcame adversity through leadership.

That's when I knew that coaching was my purpose.

Coaching Is Like Combat

A football team isn't so different from a Marine squad. Players wear helmets instead of Kevlar, but the principles are the same.

High schoolers today are just like the Marines I led—same egos, same potential. They need three things:

- To know you care;

- To know you're competent;

- To be taught how to live and lead like warriors.

In the Marines, you don't cut a teammate. You build him. You sharpen strengths, improve weaknesses, and hold the standard.

Just like in the Marines, coaching means building up the team you have.

You lead.

This Book Is for Leaders

Whether you're a coach, father, veteran, executive, warrior, mentor, or just someone seeking purpose, you're a leader.

In these pages, I draw from combat-tested experiences to shape how I lead, and how you can too. It is filled with stories, truth, and tough love. It's both a challenge and an invitation to:

- Coach like a warrior;

- Lead like a man;

- Live life with purpose.

If you are a veteran like me, wondering if your best days are behind you, they're not. The battlefield may be gone, but your mission isn't.

If you're ready to answer the call, this book will guide you step-by-step to become the kind of leader your team, family, and community needs.

Let's get to work.

Part I
Field-Proven Leadership

Chapter 1

From Battlefield to Sidelines

A Mission Renewed

This is your reminder: your strength still matters. Your mission didn't end, it just found a new field.

When I left the Marine Corps, I thought my mission was over. I had led in combat. I had trained warriors. I had given everything I had to a cause bigger than myself.

But over time, I realized something deeper was still missing: purpose.

For a while, I floated. I worked jobs. I coached a little. I went through the motions. But I felt like a part of me was still out there, still searching for a fight worth showing up for.

And then I found it again—on a football field.

Coaching Gave Me Back My Mission

The structure. The discipline. The camaraderie. The uncertainty. It all felt familiar. And more than that, it felt important.

These kids weren't just learning football; they were learning how to fight for something, how to lead, and how to live with purpose beyond the game.

And they needed someone who had been forged in fire to help shape them.

Why Veterans Make Great Coaches

If you've led in combat, you can lead in a locker room. If you've navigated hardship, you can walk with kids through their pain. If you've served something bigger than yourself, you're already equipped to serve again, this time through mentorship.

Veterans understand:

- Mission;

- Commitment;

- Brotherhood;

- Mental toughness;

- Leadership under pressure.

Coaching gives all of that a new home.

Your Next Mission Starts Here

Too many veterans think their best leadership days are behind them and that they've already given their greatest years.

But I disagree.

Your mission has changed, but your strength hasn't. You still have the fire. You still have the discipline. You still have the edge.

Now it's time to use them.

What These Kids Need

They need presence. They need patience. They need to hear where you've been, what you've overcome, and how you've come through it stronger.

Not every kid has a warrior in their life, but you can be one. And when you do it long enough, something amazing happens:

You start to heal, too.

Because in serving them, you remember who you are. In leading them, you rediscover your strength. In mentoring them, you relight your purpose.

That is what coaching gave back to me.

I lace up my boots and walk back onto that field because my mission didn't end with the Corps. It just found a new battlefield.

Chapter 2

Baptism by Fire

Lessons from Combat

Right now, you're stepping into the fire. This is where the mission begins—not when things go right, but when pressure closes in.

Combat does not just talk—it demands. There is no scoreboard, no second half, no timeouts. In the Marines, I quickly learned that rank does not automatically make you a leader, actions do. When bullets fly, the question is not just, "What's the plan?" It's also, "Can I trust the person giving orders?"

First Mission as a Leader

I will never forget my first mission as a leader in combat. We were in Afghanistan, sweeping through a town known for insurgent activity. It was hot, dusty, and eerily quiet. My heart raced, sweat poured down, and my senses heightened.

We had rehearsed these movements hundreds of times. But now, one mistake could cost lives. As a leader, my responsibility was not just my survival, it was making sure the men next to me survived. Every decision I made was a test of trust. Could my team rely on me?

That day, we followed protocol precisely and never took fire. We returned safely, not just surviving, but unified. We moved as one, watching each other's backs. I saw it in their eyes when we returned to base: they trusted me.

A few weeks later, following an IED strike during a patrol in Afghanistan, a young Marine froze under pressure. I saw fear in him, looking at a seriously injured fellow Marine rather than covering the flank.

Instinctively, I moved to his side and shouted clearly, above the noise, "Look at me. Breathe. They are getting him to the Medical Evacuation [MEDEVAC]. Do your job, he's going to be fine."

In that moment, his eyes shifted from panic to confidence. He regained his focus, covered the flank, and completed the mission alongside the platoon. Later, he told me those few words pulled him back and helped him focus on the mission.

That was when I truly understood what leadership looked like in emotional fire, something I'd see again in a different uniform, under the lights on a football field.

On the Football Field

One game, during a timeout, a defensive back came to me and asked to be removed from the game. He said he just couldn't think and was going to keep getting beat by the opposing team's wide receivers.

I saw he was overwhelmed and told him to breathe for a minute, just like I had done in moments of combat-induced panic. (Football players have a somewhat easier time doing so, in the absence of bullets whizzing overhead!)

I asked him, "Have they run anything other than the plays you saw in practice this week?" He answered, "No."

I asked, "Do you think they are faster or more athletic than you?" He answered again, "No."

I told him, "Then just go out and have fun. Don't think too much. Trust that we did everything we could to prepare you for this."

His expression changed, his eyes lit up, and he said, "Coach, you're right. I got this."

In that moment, you could see that he regained confidence and was locked back in. He intercepted a pass a few plays later and gave me a big hug when he came back to the sidelines.

In those moments, sometimes all a young man needs is a calm voice and clear direction to help him reset and refocus.

The One That Got Away

Not every kid you try to help wants to be helped.

A player I coached had the raw physical tools, but his attitude clashed with everything we taught. I pulled him aside multiple times. Gave him my number. Spoke with his parents. Tried different ways to reach him: firm talks, praise, accountability. Nothing stuck. He walked out of practices, skipped film, and eventually quit mid-season.

That one stung. I'd be lying if I said it didn't feel like failure. I replayed it in my head—what else could I have said? Should I have been tougher? More patient?

Sometimes, you plant seeds that don't take root right away. And still, the job is to keep showing up for the next kid who needs you.

Leadership isn't just about wins. It's about faith in the process.

Earned, Not Given

The Marines didn't give me leadership—they demanded it.

I had to earn respect. Not with yelling. Not with ego. But by showing up day in and day out, holding the standard, and putting my team before myself.

What separates warriors from everyone else?

It's the mindset.

We prepare with intensity. We expect adversity. And when it hits, we don't flinch. We lead through it.

Leadership Doesn't Care About Rank

One of the most defining leadership lessons of my life came not in Afghanistan, but during training.

I was a lance corporal when I was selected to attend the Infantry Squad Leaders Course (ISLC). Most of the men there were corporals or sergeants. I was young, but I'd been sharpened by strong mentors and thrown into the fire early. That course was the hardest thing I've ever done, mentally and physically.

ISLC was no joke. You were expected to lead from the front, know every tactic, and operate under intense pressure. Late in the course, we ran a scenario inside the infantry immersion trainer, a hyperrealistic mock-up of a Middle Eastern village, complete with role players, buildings, and pressure using paint rounds. The idea was simple: run a combat patrol with live actors and real consequences for bad decisions. It tested everything we'd learned.

Right before it was my turn to lead the patrol, I noticed someone quietly observing in the back. I recognized him immediately. A legendary Marine general, highly respected, battle-tested, and known for showing up where it mattered. He hadn't announced himself, and he clearly didn't want to be a distraction. But I saw him, and it rattled me.

We kicked off the mission and immediately began taking contact. I locked in. I established inner and outer cordons, pushed orders to my team leaders, and initiated a breach. We cleared the target building, neutralized the threats, and exfiltrated clean. I was proud of how we executed. It felt like a win.

Then came the After Action Review.

The instructors gave me a strong evaluation. They said I had been clear, decisive, and calm under fire. But then the general stood up.

He introduced himself to the class, and then turned his attention to me.

"You did well," he said. "But you missed something important. You didn't give me any orders."

I stood there confused.

He continued: "If you're the leader, then you're the leader. It doesn't matter what rank I am. On that patrol, I was under your command. Rank goes out the window when the mission starts. You lead everyone, or you lead no one."

That moment stopped me cold. He was absolutely right.

I had let his presence intimidate me. I had assumed, subconsciously, that his authority overrode mine. But it didn't. During that mission, I was responsible for every man on that patrol—including him.

Then he said something that burned into my soul:

"I didn't come here to watch a dog and pony show. I came to see how the MEN train."

And then:

"I put my pants on one leg at a time, just like all of you."

That moment left a permanent mark on me. Not just because of what I learned about leadership, but because of what I saw in him.

Here was a general with nothing to prove. A legend. Yet he was humble, hungry to learn, and intentional with his words. He could have embarrassed me. Instead, he made it a teaching moment for everyone. He modeled exactly what real leadership looks like: quiet strength, unshakable presence, and a commitment to the mission over ego.

That experience didn't just sharpen my mindset; it shaped how I lead to this day. Because whether it's combat, coaching, or fatherhood, this truth always holds: If you're the one called to lead, then lead. No excuses. No fear. No hesitation.

What This Means for Coaching

When I coach football now, I see the same principles play out. You don't lead because you have a whistle; you lead because your players believe in you. You earn trust daily by being reliable, present, and consistent. You go to clinics, read books, and network with other coaches in the offseason to be knowledgeable and competent in your profession. You lead from the front, never asking more than you're willing to give.

That lesson was forged in a town thousands of miles from home, as I wore cammies instead of a headset. But it applies just as much in the locker room, on the practice field, and in the lives of young men trying to find their way.

Because here's the truth: The way you lead in conflict reveals the kind of leader you really are.

And uncertainty doesn't just exist on the battlefield. It lives in broken or troubled homes. In angry teenage hearts. In the confusion of growing up in the digital age, where anything you post could go viral. There's more pressure on kids to perform now than ever before.

That's where we come in.

Chapter 3
Thriving Under Pressure
Training Mental Toughness

You've learned the mindset; now you'll train your players to lead through adversity, stay locked in, and execute when it counts.

As discussed in the combat stories earlier, pressure reveals character. Here, we'll translate that into coaching tactics that prepare athletes to handle stress.

In combat, pressure isn't a feeling, it's reality. Every decision is immediate. There are no do-overs, no second chances. You either execute or you fail. And failure can cost lives.

One of the most important lessons I learned in the Marine Corps is this: How you prepare is how you'll perform, especially when it matters most.

Combat Does Not Care About Excuses

I remember being out on patrol in an area of Afghanistan where trouble could come from any direction. We had hit IEDs and taken small-arms fire there before, but this time the intel was different.

Vague reports came through about a possible sniper hide. This sniper had already wounded several members of our unit, and we wanted badly to take him out. It wasn't just about revenge; it was about protecting our brothers. Getting him before he got another one of us.

We moved through the area knowing every rooftop, window, and doorway could be a threat. The sun was punishing, the gear was heavy, and the tension was thick. No one said it aloud, but we all knew: We were being watched.

In moments like that, the training takes over. Your heart's pounding, your mind is screaming at you to be careful, but you move with discipline, with purpose, with precision. Because the second you let fear or hesitation in, someone could die.

That is pressure.

And that is where you learn what kind of leader you really are. Not when things go as planned, but when you are staring down the unknown and your team is counting on you to make the next call.

We finished that patrol without contact, but that was not the win. The win was composure. Unity. Trust. Everyone did their job under pressure, and everyone came home.

We were ready for pressure. We expected it. And because of that, we did not flinch.

Pressure in Coaching Is Real, Too

Now, let's be real: Coaching high school football is not life or death. Even if it feels like it is for some kids.

The fourth quarter of a close game. A college scout, family, maybe a girlfriend watching from the bleachers. All eyes on them. All the pressure.

And here's the truth: If they have not been trained for pressure, they will fold under it—which is where we come in.

How I Train Mental Toughness

I coach my players the same way we trained in the Corps: Stress. Reps. Standards. Intensity. More pressure. More purpose.

Here's how:

1. **Create Controlled Conflict.** We simulate pressure in practice. Sudden changes. No-huddle drives. Loud music playing and coaches screaming. Unexpected challenges. I want them to get flustered, feel the heat, then execute anyway. Just like in combat, you rise or fall to your level of training.

2. **Teach Recovery Under Fire.** I teach them how to reset between plays. Deep breath. Clear mind. Lock back in. These are tools Marines use constantly to foster composure through breathing, posture, and mindset. If you can't recover, you can't lead.

3. **Hold the Line.** We don't lower standards when pressure rises. We raise our intensity to meet it. Players learn that success isn't about feelings, it's about execution. They do not get a pass because the lights are bright, or the moment is big. They rise or they get replaced.

From Fearful to Focused

A player I coached had big talent but a soft mentality. Every time the game got close, he would shrink. You could see it in his body language, in his eyes. He was afraid to fail.

So, I didn't yell. I didn't bench him. I leaned in.

I pulled him aside and said, "You will face pressure regularly in life. It is your proving ground. Did you say you want to be great? Then stop hoping for easy. Start owning the hard moments."

We started training differently at practice. More pressure reps. One-on-one mental toughness drills; I'd hurl insults at him and cheat in the drills to make him frustrated. Then we'd perform the drill regularly and allow him to win despite his frustration.

We visualized game situations. Slowly, he stopped fearing failure and started facing it.

He became dependable—focused, steady, and confident when it mattered most. It reinforced to me early in my career that we needed to train more mental toughness if our program was going to take the next steps.

What You Model, They Mirror

As the leader—coach, veteran, or father—you are the thermostat. If you panic, they panic. If you stay calm, they follow your lead.

So, when the moment is big, when the lights are bright, when the team's behind and the crowd is loud—these moments don't make you a leader. They confirm the leader you've already trained to be, and they're when your preparation is proven.

When your players see that in you, they will start believing they can do it too.

Ready to lead under pressure?

Teach them to reset, refocus, and rise when it matters most.

My Go-To Drill: Cadence Under Pressure

Step 1: Discuss during a water break the importance of mental toughness.

Example: "Good teams can perform at game time. But the great teams, the ones who win championships, can still focus and perform under pressure at critical moments. If we want to be the type of team that wins the big games, then we must be able to focus and perform no matter how tired we are and how much pressure is on us."

Step 2: Go through a team workout until most of the team is visibly exhausted.

I use sprints, sleds, running the hill next to our practice field, or some combination for this.

Step 3: We line up along the end line. I remind our players that they must to learn to perform under pressure and while exhausted to reach our goals. I remind them to take a deep breath and clear their minds.

We then perform a cadence drill the length of the field and for every rep that someone goes offsides we will do another hill as a team following the drill.

CADENCE DRILL

The entire team lines up on the end line of the field in their offensive position stance.

The quarterback announces what cadence the ball will be snapped on, and then the team repeats it aloud.

The quarterback then calls his cadence from shotgun with the center five yards in front of him.

On the snap of the ball, the entire team sprints forward 10 yards and then backward five yards. They then immediately get back in their offensive stance and repeat.

This takes the team forward five yards every rep until they reach the opposite end line.

Mental Prep Checklist

Ask yourself if you're doing the following:

- Goal-setting with my athletes;

- Addressing self-talk and giving "how-to";

- Teaching visualization;

- Teaching breathing techniques;

- Creating uncertainty and challenge in practice;

- Simulating realistic high-pressure moments;

- Fostering positive feedback between players.

I'll end with this:

- What percentage of the game do you think is mental?

- Now, what percentage of your practice is mental?

Chapter 4
The Warrior Ethos
Core Values for Leadership

This is your foundation. Before you lead others, you must live the values that make a Warrior Coach unshakable.

As we established in the introduction, leadership begins with self-discipline.

In the Marine Corps, we did not just learn how to shoot, move, and communicate. We were trained relentlessly to live by a set of values that defined who we were as men and warriors. These values were not just posters on a wall or empty slogans in a handbook. They were expectations, enforced by the brother next to you and the standard set before you.

Leadership starts with who you are when no one is watching. That is the Warrior way. And it is built on the values that every Marine— and every coach, father, or leader— should embody.

INTEGRITY

Do what's right, especially when it is hard.

Integrity in the Marines was not optional. It meant owning your mistakes, telling the truth even when it hurt, holding the line even when no one else did. In coaching, integrity means keeping your word to your players, showing up on time, and leading by example every day.

Trust isn't earned by what you say, it's built in the moments you show up, stay steady, and follow through.

I set the example for our team by owning my mistakes. For instance, we lost a game my first year as head coach because I decided to roll the dice and go for it on fourth down trying to ice the game, rather than punting the ball and playing field position. This allowed the opposing team to have a short field and score to win.

After the game, during our team talk, I took responsibility and told the team, "The loss rests on my shoulders. I was overly aggressive, and I own that."

INITIATIVE

Do not wait to be told—get it done.

The best Marines do not sit around waiting for orders. They see what needs to be done and do it. As a coach, I expect the same. Fix your own problems. Pick up the trash on the field. Step in when another coach is struggling. Lead your position group like it's your military unit.

Initiative is the spark. It drives momentum, builds confidence, and helps you win long before game day.

When I'm walking around the practice field, the game field, the campus, even the town, I let players see me bending down to pick up trash.

I reward players who show up early and start doing drills on their own at pre-practice.

I give time to players who want to stay after practice and get better.

ENTHUSIASM

Bring energy, even when it is uncomfortable.

Some days, enthusiasm is easy. Others, it is a choice. I have patrolled through 100-degree heat in full gear with zero sleep and still found a way to crack a joke, hype up my guys, or flash a grin. Why? Because morale matters.

If your team sees you dragging, they drag. But if they see you fired up, they follow. Bring the energy.

I allow music at my practices (so long as it doesn't become a distraction). And I even break out some dance moves every now and then!

I do whatever it takes to keep the energy high, because the team feeds off it.

BEARING

Hold yourself with discipline, control, and presence.

Your bearing is your posture, your composure, your command presence. Marines are taught to carry themselves like professionals: clean, sharp, locked-in. You should look like a leader before you speak.

Your bearing sets the tone, and players can feel it. They will follow your body language long before they follow your play calls.

For example, if you complain about the officiating, players will complain. I have a policy that only I get to talk to officials. And if I, or any of my staff, hear a player complain, we shut it down immediately.

We have made our mindset "bring it on." This means we will continue fighting no matter what is thrown at us. If we have to play at a disadvantage, then it makes the victory that much sweeter!

UNSELFISHNESS

Put the mission and the men before yourself.

This was burned into us early as Marines. You eat last. You clean up first. You give credit to others. You take the blame when it is needed. It's not about being a martyr, it's about being a servant leader.

On a football team, that looks like giving your players the spotlight. It means staying after practice to help a struggling lineman and making sacrifices they will never see, because that is what real leaders do.

COURAGE

Do the hard thing. Especially when you're scared.

Courage is not the absence of fear; it is acting in spite of it. In combat, fear is always present. But courage means pushing forward anyway, because your brothers are counting on you.

In life, courage is telling someone they are out of line, or calling out laziness on your team, or pulling a player aside to hold him accountable when it would be easier to just ignore it.

This may mean making a tough change on your staff for the good of the team, even though you don't want to hurt anyone's feelings.

Courage creates change.

LOYALTY

Have their backs. No matter what.

In the Marines, loyalty meant you would go through hell for your team. I carry that into every locker room. You stand up for your players. And you never talk about your squad behind their backs. You protect your coaches. Always address problems head-on, speak to others face to face. Whatever happens, once you leave the office (or the locker room), it stays there.

Even the smallest crack in loyalty can damage team unity, which is why I emphasize it constantly. I ask questions about loyalty when interviewing coaches for my staff. I regularly talk about loyalty and how to handle disagreements within my staff.

Loyalty builds trust. Trust builds teams. Teams win. These tenets cannot be overemphasized.

FAIRNESS

Hold everyone to the same standard.

It doesn't matter if it is your best player or the kid who rides the bench: Every man gets the same rules, the same treatment, and the same expectations. No favorites. No excuses.

If you let one guy slip, the whole standard slips. Fair does not mean soft. Fair means firm and equal.

Values Tested

During our first game week, one of our best players missed practice. He knew the rule—if you are absent, you do not start. Despite his talent, I benched him for the first quarter.

Many expected I would let it slide because of his talent. But after the game, the player approached me in the locker room and said, "Coach, I get it. I will be there from here on out." From that day forward, he was not just there—he became a leader in punctuality and accountability, reinforcing our team's integrity.

Conclusion

These values protect you, define your leadership, and guide every decision you make. When you lead with them, your team will follow, even through fire.

And when you don't, they will know. Players can smell fake leadership from a mile away. But when they see a man who walks the walk, lives the values, and leads with strength and purpose, they will run through a wall for him.

That is the Warrior Coach.

Self-Reflection Exercise

Rate yourself in the categories below. 1=Poor, 2=Below Average, 3=Average, 4=Above Average, 5=Great

Integrity _____

Initiative _____

Enthusiasm _____

Bearing _____

Unselfishness _____

Courage _____

Loyalty _____

Fairness _____

TOTAL _____

If you scored any 1 or 2, you need to continue striving to find ways to improve your skills before becoming a leader.

If you scored 3, 4, and 5, you are on your way to becoming a successful leader.

If you scored all 4's and 5's you have honed your skills as a leader; continue learning and consider mentoring new leaders.

Chapter 5

Becoming the Warrior Coach

Leadership Defined

This is the transformation point. You're no longer just reacting, you're building men.

A Warrior Coach is not just someone with a clipboard and a whistle. He is someone who has been through fire, endured failure, and led when the stakes were highest. He has been battle-tested in life and is now stepping up to lead the next generation with strength, clarity, and purpose.

I do not coach football because I love the X's and O's (although I do). I coach because I have seen what happens when young men grow up with no guidance, no direction, and no one holding the standard.

I have seen them in combat. And I have seen them in classrooms. They are the same.

Young men today are starving for leadership and discipline. They need someone to show them how to act, how to speak, and how to carry themselves like warriors in a world that wants to keep them soft, distracted, and weak.

The Warrior Coach stands in that gap.

He says: "Follow me. We don't lower the standard. You're capable of more, and I'm going to pull it out of you."

What Makes a Warrior Coach Different?

While most coaches chase wins, Warrior Coaches chase something bigger: They build men. Warrior Coaches lead with clarity and purpose before the emotional fire begins. Warrior Coaches stay locked in under fire. This echoes the earlier distinction between reaction and readiness.

They build culture, enforce standards, and develop character. And they do it without apology.

The Men Who Shaped Me

Two leaders in the Marine Corps changed the way I understood leadership forever.

The first was a gunnery sergeant who was intense, loud, and deliberate. When he raised his voice, it wasn't out of anger. It was intentional. He used intensity like a tool to snap us to attention, to cut through fear, or to ignite fire in us when we needed it most. He never yelled just to yell. His energy was focused, and his corrections were sharp. I respected him deeply, because he was consistent, fair, and fiercely committed to making us better.

The second was a master sergeant I worked under later in my career. He was the opposite in tone—quiet, calm, and 10 steps ahead of everyone in the room. He didn't need to raise his voice. His leadership came through in the details. In his presence. In how he never missed a beat, never overlooked a Marine who needed mentorship, and never let standards slip. He was brilliant, and he led with a quiet strength that made you want to rise to his level.

Both of these men influenced my coaching style. One taught me how to lead with command presence and energy. The other showed me how to lead with mentorship, poise, and quiet authority. Together, they gave me the blueprint for becoming the kind of leader who can both challenge and uplift in all areas: the locker room, at home, and in life.

My Personal Standard: How I Live and Coach

I lead my team with five non-negotiables:

1. Communication

Clear, direct, consistent. No mixed messages. Everyone knows what is expected and what is not tolerated. This includes parents. Open communication builds trust, alignment, and respect. If they know what you stand for, they will be more likely to stand with you when things get tough.

2. Consistency

Bring the same energy, discipline, and leadership every day, whether we're up by 40 or getting punched in the mouth. Minimize the pressure for your team.

3. Brotherhood

A football team is a family. We protect each other, fight for each other, and hold each other accountable, just like a squad in combat.

4. Loyalty

I have your back; you'd better have mine. You must maintain unity and trust in your staff. We stay unified; no gossip, no fractures, no hidden agendas. That does not mean I will go easy on you, but it means I will not leave you behind. Ever.

5. Care

I genuinely care about every one of my players as young men first. Before I coach them, I mentor them. I check in. I hold the line because I care. They may not always like it, but they'll always know I've got their backs.

From Whistle to Weapon

When I coach, I do not see a game, I see a mission. I am there to train boys to become men who will lead their families, serve their communities, and show up when it matters.

That starts with me.

Warrior Coaches model toughness, earn respect through action, and stay committed, even when their players are ready to give up.

This world needs more people willing to step up and make a difference. It needs leaders on a mission. And that is exactly who we are.

Defining Your Leadership Exercise

What standards are your non-negotiables as a leader?

What do you do to meet each standard?

How can you improve your standards? What new standards would you like to set?

Chapter 6

Discipline and Consistency

Setting the Standard

Here, you'll cement your program's identity, through daily standards, structure, and modeling.

Without discipline, talent is wasted. Without standards, conflict takes over. Without consistency, culture crumbles.

If you want a program that lasts, you must build it on structure, not hype. Hype gets you fired up for a day. Discipline shapes you for life.

Live your leadership values every day

I never ask a player to do something I will not do myself.

If I tell them to be early, I am early. If I demand effort, I bring effort. If I preach toughness, I live it.

Standards aren't taught from a playbook, they're proven by example. If you stop modeling them, your players will too.

Inspect What You Expect

This is one of the most important leadership habits I have brought from the Marine Corps into coaching.

If you say you care about discipline, then check the little things: how they warm up, carry their gear, and how they treat the locker room. If you say effort matters, then coach it. Do not let laziness slide, and do not tolerate excuses.

Inspect what you expect, every day, because players only take a standard seriously if you do.

Example:

We had players forgetting gear for games, so I instituted a military-style gear check in the locker room before each away game. Each player had to lay all gear out neatly in front of their locker as if it was a player lying on the ground. Coaches then checked off each item and watched them pack it one by one. This ended our issues in a hurry.

Consistency Is King

The most dangerous coach in any program is the inconsistent one.

The one who is fiery one day and checked out the next. The one who praises effort on Monday, then ignores laziness on Wednesday. That kind of leadership destroys trust.

Consistency doesn't mean perfection—it means showing up with the same focus and values every day, no matter the score or the storm.

That is how players learn to depend on you. That is how they learn to depend on themselves.

Demand Effort, Not Perfection

I do not expect my players to be perfect. I expect them to bring it.

Bringing it means showing up ready to work, finishing sprints, grinding through tough drills, and pushing forward even when your body begs you to quit.

And when they don't, I call it out.

Not to embarrass them. But because effort is the one thing they control, and it is the one thing that will carry them through life when nothing else is going right.

High Standards Build High Character

You do not just shape a football team by enforcing discipline. You shape men.

Because when a young man learns to be on time, keep his word, respect his coaches, finish his work, and own his mistakes, he is learning how to lead a household, make a mark in his career path, and serve a cause bigger than himself.

That is what we are building. And it all starts with standards.

A Story of Standards in Action

In my first year as head coach, we were on the road, battling in a tight game against a tough opponent. We had closed the gap to one score in the third quarter. Our sideline was fired up. Momentum was swinging our way.

I had a junior on the team who was a talented leader and a game-changer. But like a lot of young men with raw talent, he struggled with emotional control. Passion isn't a problem; undisciplined emotion is.

On a critical fourth-and-five near midfield, their offense lined up trying to draw us offsides. Everyone on our sideline was screaming, "Watch the ball!" but in the heat of the moment, he jumped. Offsides. First down.

He was angry. I yelled to him, "Lock in! Own the next play!" But the pressure mounted. On the very next snap, a questionable call went against us. Instead of staying composed, he snapped and said something to the official, drawing a 15-yard unsportsmanlike penalty.

I called him over to talk.

But he didn't just ignore me; he shouted back, "I'm the best player on your team!" and walked away.

Right then, I made a decision: I pulled him from the field, took his helmet, and told him he was done for the night.

He kept insisting we couldn't win without him. And maybe he was right, but we went on to tie the game and lost in the final seconds.

The real loss would have been letting that behavior slide. Because in our program, no one—not even the best player—is above the standard. Every player is expected to lead with respect, discipline, and team-first values. Always.

It was a hard moment. But I do not coach for comfort, I coach for character.

After the game, and once the emotions settled, we had a few tough conversations. One-on-one mentoring. No yelling. Just man-to-man. In time, that same young man came into my office, looked me in the eye, hugged me, and said, "It won't happen again, Coach."

That's when I knew the lesson had landed. And it reminded me why I do this.

Winning games is great. But helping a young man grow into someone he's proud of is the real win.

Scenario Exercise

Let's say you have a star player named Jimmy who's been late three days in a row. You know your assistant coaches have already spoken to him, but today, you're going to address the problem directly.

What are two important messages you will convey to him when you start the conversation?

What is the first thing you would ask him?

Jimmy blames transportation issues and says it won't happen again. But he's late again the following week. What steps will you take to hold him accountable?

Exercise Sample Answers

Let's say you have a star player named Jimmy who's been late three days in a row. You know your assistant coaches have already spoken to him, but today, you're going to address the problem directly.

What are two important messages you will convey to him when you start the conversation?

I would reiterate the standards that every member of our team agreed to. I would also add that to be a leader, he is expected to set the example for the rest of the team.

What is the first thing you would ask him?

I would ask for the reason he's late and how I can help fix the problem.

Jimmy blames transportation issues and says it won't happen again. But he's late again the following week. What steps will you take to hold him accountable?

I would hold Jimmy to the same expectations of anyone on my team, meaning that he wouldn't start the game. I would wait at least one full series before putting him in, and he also would not be representing our team as a captain. He would have to earn back that honor.

Part II
Developing Men

Chapter 7

Leading the Difficult Player

Every coach, at some point, will face a challenge that isn't about X's and O's, but character, chemistry, and conflict. This is the test of your leadership: can you develop the kid who doesn't make it easy to be coached?

Why Difficult Players Matter

The easy players don't foster growth in coaches. The difficult ones do.

They challenge your patience, sharpen your standards, and force you to evolve as a leader. And they're the often ones who need you the most.

Behind every "problem kid" is a story: pain, pressure, pride, or survival. And while not every one of them will turn the corner, the way you lead them *always* matters.

Common Types of Difficult Players

The Talented Rebel: Gifted, but doesn't respect authority

The Victim Mindset: Blames others, avoids responsibility

The Quiet Resister: Nods in meetings, checks out in games

The Entitled Star: Thinks the rules don't apply to him

The Wounded Fighter: Defensive because of life outside football

Each one requires a different approach, but they all require leadership.

Principles to Lead Difficult Players

1. See the Person First

Ask yourself: Who is he outside the helmet?

Ask about home life, siblings, school.

First, listen more than you speak.

You can't coach a player you haven't earned the right to challenge.

2. Set the Standard—Then Stick to It

Don't lower expectations because they're difficult.

The standard must be clear, consistent, and enforced without apology.

The team is always watching how you respond.

3. Find the Leverage Point

Every player has something they care about:

Is it playing time?

Earning respect?

Being seen?

Escaping home stress?

Find what drives them, and tie your coaching to that purpose.

4. Correct in Private, Celebrate in Public

Never embarrass them in front of peers if you can avoid it.

Pull them aside and be firm when they need to be corrected. Then affirm any positive progress in front of the team.

5. Give Them a Leadership Opportunity

It may seem counterintuitive, but giving difficult players small leadership moments (like leading stretches or mentoring a younger player) can begin to shift their identity from rebel to role model.

Real Example: *The Player Who Tested Everything*

I once coached a kid who had raw talent but challenged every drill, every decision, every boundary.

He skipped lifts. Talked back. Perhaps worst of all, he laughed when teammates were held accountable.

My assistants were ready to cut him. But I decided to take a different approach.

One day, after a particularly frustrating practice, I told him, "Enough is enough. I'm not going to be constantly undermined and have you acting like everything is a joke. These younger kids look up to you. Start acting like a senior and lead the team. Prove you can do it this week with every stretch, every lift, every hill, every meeting. Then we'll talk."

He didn't like it, but he responded by showing up on time three days straight, which had never happened before.

So, I gave him a job: mentoring our sophomore quarterback. It wasn't magic, but it started a shift. He saw himself differently. He began to *own* instead of resist.

Was it perfect? No. He still had his moments.

But he finished the season stronger, and that's what this work is about.

What to Remember

You won't win them all. But you can always lead with consistency.

Don't coach for comfort; coach for growth.

Never let one player diminish your team's culture, but don't give up on them too early either.

Every kid is a battlefield of potential and pain.

You don't need to win the war in one day. Just stay in the fight.

That's what Warrior Coaches do.

Chapter 8

Forging Brotherhood

Building Unbreakable Team Culture

Now you shift from individual leader to culture builder. This is where teams become tribes.

You can't win without talent, but you can't lead without culture.

Every team has players. Not every team has brotherhood. And that is the difference between a group of athletes and a unit of warriors.

Brotherhood is not just something you hope for. It's something you build through intent, example, and unbreakable standards.

Show Them You Care Before You Coach

This is the first rule of team culture.

If your players don't believe you care about them as men, they will not follow you as a coach. They may show up and participate, but they won't give you their all unless they know you care.

I start every season with personal conversations. One-on-ones. I want to know what is going on at home, what burdens they're carrying, what they are fighting through. Some don't have strong parents in the picture. Others don't eat outside of school. Some are just trying to hold it together.

And if I am going to demand everything from them on the field, I'd better show them they matter off of it.

Culture Is Built Daily

Brotherhood does not happen at the end of the season; it starts on day one.

Every practice, every meeting, and every rep has chances to shape the culture. And that culture must be built on discipline, accountability, and care.

Here's how I do it:

Set the Standard, Then Enforce It. We do not have an overabundance of rules, but some are non-negotiable. We show up on time. We finish our reps. We clean up after ourselves. And we do not let our teammates slack. Culture starts to crack the moment you overlook a standard.

Make It Hard—Intentionally. We build shared struggles into the program. Early-morning lifts in the offseason. Team conditioning throughout the summer and at practice. Challenging drills that test grit, effort, and unity. Comfort doesn't connect people, shared struggle does. When players sweat, suffer, and overcome together, they form a bond that cannot be faked. In the Marines we say, "Misery builds camaraderie."

Create Real Accountability. If a player or coach is slacking, we call it out. We teach them to police their own teammates, because peer-to-peer accountability is stronger than anything we say. And when a leader emerges from within the ranks, we fan that flame. The team is always player-led.

This family. Period.

I tell my team: "You do not have to like each other, but you will respect each other. You will fight for each other. And when it is hard, you do not run. You dig deeper."

Some things we do:

Ladies Football Camp: during the summer: BYOB and learn football basics from the coaches. We follow this with a potluck dinner.

Kickoff Dinner: All families are invited to bring a dish to pass and enjoy dinner while getting to know players, staff, and other families at the end of the first week of practice.

Weekly Team Dinners: Players, coaches, and the cheer team all eat dinner together the night before each game, an event organized by our "Mom Squad."

Playoff Reveal Party: We invite the whole community to join us at the school for dinner and to watch as the playoff pairings are revealed on the auditorium screen.

A Story of Brotherhood in Action

Forty-five seconds left in the fourth quarter of what's been a hard-fought game. Our opponent just scored a touchdown to go up 20–16.

Most teams would fold. Not us.

The culture we built, the brotherhood the team shared, and the challenges we had put them through in practice all showed up in that moment.

The message was simple: believe. First in yourself, then in your brothers, and then in the work you've all put in.

We started with the ball on our own 20-yard line. After two incomplete passes and three quarterback scrambles that moved the ball to our 35, the clock wound down to 20 seconds.

Then it happened: Our quarterback dropped back and hit one of our playmakers over the middle. He had the ball in space and turned it into magic. He made defenders miss, followed his blocks, and broke free for a touchdown.

22–20. 17 seconds left. Game over.

That win wasn't about luck; it was the product of brotherhood forged in the fire of shared struggle and bonded by belief.

A team built on talent alone will fall apart when things get tough. But a team built on brotherhood becomes dangerous, because they are playing for something bigger than themselves, and they become unbreakable.

Culture Checklist

Does my culture include:

- Team members feeling valued;

- Team members feeling a sense of belonging ;

- Team members feeling comfortable coming to me with problems;

- Team members feel treated equally;

- Team members encouraging each other;

- Team members knowing their role;

- Challenging practices;

- Competitive drills;

- Knowing every team member's personal situation;

- Knowing what drives each member of my team;

- Knowing the learning styles of my team;

- Regular communication with parents.

Chapter 9
Leading Assistant Coaches

A Warrior Coach is only as strong as the team around him, including his assistant coaches. If you want a high-performing program built on trust and excellence, you must be intentional about how you lead the men coaching with you, not just the players you're coaching.

Set the Standard Early
Your assistants need clarity, not confusion. They don't need to guess what kind of staff they've joined. Set the tone immediately:

- What are your non-negotiables?

- What's your communication rhythm?

- What kind of example should they be setting on and off the field?

Early in my career, I made the mistake of assuming everyone would just "get it." But when you assume, you create gaps, and gaps create friction. When I started communicating clearly and consistently, our staff chemistry changed overnight.

Give Them Ownership
Micromanagement kills morale. If you want your assistants to lead with fire, give them space to own their roles.

When I assign a position group, I make it clear: "This is your group. Own it. Develop it. Be accountable for it."

But ownership doesn't mean absence. I check in. I observe. I coach my coaches. And when something's off, I correct it respectfully—but directly.

Empowered assistants become invested assistants. And that investment always shows up on the field.

Correct Behind Closed Doors, Sing Praise In Public

There will be moments when your assistants fall short. It happens. But how you handle those moments defines your culture.

If something goes wrong, pull them aside. Speak plainly, not punitively. Say what needs to be said, but do it with the same respect you expect from them.

Then, when they get it right—when they grind, innovate, or lead well—praise them where others can hear. That builds loyalty. That builds confidence.

Build Brotherhood, Not Just Staff

Your coaching staff isn't just a group of employees. It's a team of leaders who shape young men. The tighter your bond, the more unified your message.

Invest in your assistants like you do your players:

- Host regular staff dinners;

- Check in on their families;

- Encourage collaboration, not competition.

I've seen staffs fall apart because of ego, insecurity, or silence. Don't let that happen. Set a tone of humility and brotherhood from the top.

Multiply the Mission

When you lead your assistants well, your impact multiplies. Suddenly it's not just you coaching leadership, discipline, and toughness—it's a team of men doing it together. And that's how championship cultures are built.

You don't just coach players. You coach coaches. And when you do that well, your legacy grows far beyond the field.

Chapter 10
Breaking Barriers
Pushing Past Limits

This is the breaking point—and the breakthrough. You'll help your players find grit beyond their comfort zones.

Most young men do not know how far they can go, because no one has ever pushed them to find out.

They have been taught to stay comfortable. To avoid the hard stuff. And as a result, too many of them grow up physically soft, mentally weak, and spiritually lost.

Those traits do not fly in my program. We are going to find your limits and then challenge them regularly. We are even going to ask you to do things that we know you can't do, just to see how far you can push yourself. This is the only way to truly reach your potential.

Discomfort Is the Way

In the Marines, we learned early that pain is a teacher.

You do not grow by staying in your safe zone. You grow by pushing through it. A forced march in 110-degree heat, a combat patrol on no sleep, a training scenario where everything is going wrong—these moments forge a toughness that can't be taught in a classroom.

Discomfort sharpens toughness in a way no classroom ever could. And that is exactly what I create in my coaching environment.

Push Their Physical Limits. We run. We lift. We condition hard. But I do not just make them work to get stronger; I make them work to understand that the body is limited by the mind. When they think they're finished, I prove there's more in the tank—because there almost always is. Because in this program, we believe one simple truth: Challenge builds camaraderie, because nothing bonds teams like shared suffering.

Break Comfort Patterns. We challenge routines—on purpose. Sudden changes in conditioning circuits, mixing A's and B's in practice reps, loud and chaotic environments with music playing and coaches screaming. Why? Because I want them to learn to adjust on the fly, to stay sharp, and to lead in uncertainty—not just when it is scripted. That's how you build warriors, not just players.

Build Mental Reps. I don't wait for the fourth quarter to test our focus. We manufacture pressure in practice. I push the team until the mental fog sets in, which is when we go no-huddle. We run cadence drills when we're tired, we rep plays at full speed, and we train their brains to function in fatigue. If you want your team to execute under pressure, you must train them in pressure. Create tough scenarios that could happen in a game and drill them. Treat it like it's the Super Bowl and build that pressure in practice occasionally. We talk about suffering with purpose. Visualization. Emotional reset techniques. They learn how to breathe, reset, and refocus before they ever have to do it under the lights.

The Wall Is Where Growth Starts

Every athlete hits the wall—at that moment when their legs are heavy, their lungs are on fire, and their brain is screaming to quit.

Most stop there.

Warriors keep going.

I tell my players, "Your body will do what your mind tells it. That can be that you are done, or that can be that you will not be stopped."

When you teach a young man how to break through that wall once, he learns he can do it again. And not just on the field—in life. Push athletes' limits and take them to failure, but end with a success and celebrate the effort it took. Confidence grows when they break through limits, and resilience forms when they realize they can do it again.

The Role of the Coach in the Fire

The easy thing is to pull a kid back when he is struggling. To let him cruise. To lower the weight or shorten the drill.

The Warrior Coach does the opposite. You push him forward, meet his eyes, and say, "You're not done yet." That's when you help him see who he's becoming, not who he was.

Because in that moment of decision—the choice to quit or continue—is where transformation lives. And most young men do not need sympathy in that moment. They need someone who believes in them and refuses to let them settle.

Tough Love Builds Grit

I love it when players tell me after a brutal practice: "Coach, I hated that workout—but I needed it. Thank you."

That's when you know you're doing it right.

If your players never struggle, stretch themselves beyond their perceived limits, or face hard truths, you're not coaching them—you're shielding them. But if they leave your program more disciplined, more confident, and more resilient than whe they came in, you've changed their lives.

And that is the whole mission.

Chapter 11

Tough Love Leadership

Coaching with Impact

Your leadership sharpens here. Truth. Accountability. Love with backbone. This is where boys grow into men.

Tough love is not about yelling. It's not about being a hard-ass for no reason. It's about caring enough to tell the truth, hold the line, and demand they do better.

It is love that does not flinch, but rather corrects, confronts, and pushes—because mediocrity has no place in a warrior's life.

And most young men today do not need softer voices. They need stronger leaders.

Confront It, Then Coach It

When I see laziness, bad body language, or selfish behavior, I call it out. On the spot. Not to shame them. Not to embarrass them. But to wake them up.

Because if I let it slide, I am telling the team that it's okay. And it's not. But after I call it out, I pull them in. I check in. I remind them of what they are capable. I challenge them to rise—not just for themselves, but for their brother next to them.

Get Personal, Stay Direct

I make it my mission to know each player as a man. What drives them? What wounds do they carry with them? What kind of life do they have at home?

I even do my best to attend all their games in other sport seasons, because leadership does not stop when football ends.

I give my players a hug every time I see them and they will even see me in public and give me a hug. In the military you never knew when the last time you would see someone was. We regularly embraced brothers we were close with. That may be taboo to some, but I have no problem giving those I care about a hug or receiving one, no matter what gender or age.

When your players know you see who they are—not just what they do on the field—they'll open up to real leadership.

And once they know you care deeply, they will accept the hard truths you give them.

I have told the players:

"You're just going through the motions—you're better than that." Or "Your attitude sucks. Fake it till you make it if you have to." Or even "You can be a great contributor, but not if you don't push yourself past your limitations."

And they have responded—not with anger, but with growth. Because I wasn't saying these things to them to stroke my own ego; I was saying them because I believe in them as men.

You really have to be honest with players when they come to you too. When a player asks me, "Coach, why don't I start?" I give them the brutally honest reasons, but I also give them a plan for how to earn that position.

Similarly, if a parent asks that same question, the answer should be the same. This may seem brash to some, but I have always had parents respond well to it. That doesn't mean that we always agree, but they leave knowing my rationale and how their child can earn what they want.

Coach Quietly, Celebrate Loudly

As I stated earlier, about assistant coaches, the same goes for players.

If a player steps up, if he responds to coaching, if he grows, I make sure the team sees it.

Not for his ego, but as an example, so the others know what growth looks like, and that growth is what will be rewarded.

Give away weekly effort and attitude awards, recognize the scout-team hero, and try to award them to different athletes each week.

Culture Always Outweighs Talent

One of the greatest dangers in coaching is letting a talented player get away with bad habits because you "need him to win."

But you do not win that way. Not for long. And you definitely do not build men that way.

I have benched starters for disrespect. I have pulled captains for lack of effort. I have taken helmets away during games to protect the culture of the team.

That moment reminded me of our core belief: Even the most gifted player must rise to the same standard as everyone else, because culture is built on what you consistently enforce.

Tough Love Over Time Builds Trust

I had a player once who barely spoke. He kept his head down, avoided eye contact, and resisted any form of accountability. But I stayed on him, firmly and consistently, always reminding him that I believed in who he could become.

Years later, he sent me a handwritten letter—not a text. It read, "Coach, thank you for all you did for me. You were always there for me and you helped me grow."

Some players won't thank you today. Some will resist. Some will walk away. But the ones who grow will come back with the truth.

The rewards of tough love aren't applause, popularity, or wins. They are growth, impact, and legacy.

Part III

Leading at Home

Chapter 12
More Than a Coach
Embracing Fatherhood on the Field

By now, you're more than a coach. You're a father figure. A mentor. The man they come back to later in life.

There's a difference between being a coach and being a father figure.

A coach leads drills. A father figure builds connection.

A coach teaches plays. A father figure teaches life.

A coach corrects mistakes. A father figure helps you fix them.

The Warrior Coach does all these things.

Filling the Gap

Many young men show up without a stable male figure in their life. They're not just lacking structure, they're starving for it. They need a man who is present, listens, shows up, and believes in them, especially when they're ready to give up on themselves.

I've seen the shift happen: A player who used to avoid eye contact starts seeking me out after practice. A quiet kid begins to lead warmups. A player struggling at home starts showing up early just to be in the building.

These are signs that you've become more than a coach—you've become safe for them. And for many kids, that changes everything.

What I Give My Players

I give them my time, whether it's a quick chat about school, a deeper talk about home life—or just asking how they're really doing. I check in when I see something is off. I tell them I'm proud of them, because some have never heard it from a man before. I hug them after a win—and after a loss. I give them my number and tell them to call or text anytime.

And when they do? I answer.

Because that is what a father figure does.

How They Respond

They start to open up. They ask questions. They come to you when things go wrong. They introduce you to their kids years later. They invite you to their graduation parties, and later on, their weddings.

This is the long game. This is what makes the grind worth it.

You are not just coaching for this season. You're building men for life, and they will remember how you made them feel—long after the memories of the field fade.

That's how your leadership echoes long after the final whistle.

Chapter 13
Leadership in the Home

The Warrior Coach doesn't take off the uniform when he walks through the door. Leadership doesn't end at the locker room—it begins again at home.

The First Team You Lead

Before you lead a football team, you lead your family.

Before you build culture in a locker room, you build it in your living room.

This chapter is for every man who wants to show up better for his wife, his kids, and his household. Leadership in the home is the foundation of all other leadership. If we miss it here, we miss it everywhere.

What Leadership at Home Looks Like

It's not about barking orders or having all the answers.

It's about presence, consistency, and example.

Your family watches:

- How you respond to stress

- How you treat their mother

- Whether you keep your word

- What you do when no one's watching

You don't have to be perfect, but you must be intentional.

Five Habits of a Warrior at Home

1. Start the Day with Purpose

Even five minutes of stillness, gratitude, or mental focus can shift your mindset.

- Reflect on how you want to show up today as a father, husband, and leader.

- Ask yourself: *What do my kids need from me today? What does my wife need from me today?*

2. Family Huddle Once a Week

- Sit down with your wife and/or kids for 15 minutes.

- Talk through the week about your schedule, goals, and challenges.

- Ask them, "How can I support you better this week?"

3. Lead the Energy at Home

- Your tone sets the temperature.

- Choose to bring calm, encouragement, and strength, even when you're tired.

4. Show Love with Action

- Leave a note.

- Do a chore without being asked.

- Sit on the floor and play.

- Hug your kids often, and tell them you're proud of them—not just for performance, but for who they are.

5. Model What You Want Them to Become

- If you want respectful kids, speak with respect.

- If you want a strong marriage, put your spouse's needs before your own.

- If you want responsible teens, show them what owning your responsibilities looks like.

Leadership in Marriage

Your wife doesn't need you to be a drill sergeant. She needs you to be present, supportive, and dependable.

Do this:

- Initiate hard conversations instead of avoiding them;

- Protect your time together like you protect game film;

- Ask her: "What do you need from me this week?"

- Celebrate her wins—big or small.

Warrior Coaches don't just lead when it's easy, they lead with commitment when it's hard.

When You Fail

You're going to mess this up sometimes. You're going to come home short-tempered, distracted, or emotionally empty.

Here's the key:

- **Own it. Apologize quickly. Adjust intentionally.**

Your kids don't need perfect, they need real. They need to see what humility and growth look like. That's leadership.

Sample Weekly Family Rhythm

Sunday: Review the upcoming week with your spouse; have a short family meeting with the kids.

Weekdays: Have a 10-minute one-on-one with a different kid each day; talk about school, friends, and goals.

Friday: Family dinner, no phones.

Weekend: Do one activity that fills your wife's tank and one that fills your kids' tank.

You don't need to do everything; just do *something*, consistently.

What Kids Remember

They remember if you came to their game. They remember if you cheered for them. They remember your discipline—but also your grace. They remember if they felt safe and seen.

And one day, they'll lead their families the way you led them.

Make sure you give them something worth modeling.

Final Word

Your household is your greatest coaching job.

If you never win a championship, but your son grows up to be a loving, strong, disciplined father.... If your daughter grows up knowing what respect looks like in a man.... If your wife knows she is loved, valued, and prioritized....

You win.

The world is full of strong men who failed at home.

Don't let that be your story.

Lead your family with as much focus, fire, and love as you lead your team.

Part IV
The Mission Continues

Chapter 14

First 30 Days as a Warrior Coach

You don't build a culture overnight, but you do set the tone immediately. Here's how to lead with clarity and conviction from day one.

Overview

Whether you're a brand-new head coach, an assistant stepping into more responsibility, or a father figure running a youth team, your first 30 days are where you earn trust—or lose it.

This is your blueprint.

Follow it. Adjust it to your situation. But don't wing it.

Phase 1: Days 1 through 10 – Establish Trust & Purpose
Priorities:

- Build relationships, not just authority;

- Share your mission; tell them who you are, why you coach, and what you believe;

- Set the foundation: communicate core values, team expectations, and your leadership model.

Action Steps:
1. Meet with each player individually (5–10 mins)

- Ask about family, school, and goals;

- Learn names fast; call everyone by their name on day one.

2. Open team meeting: The Warrior Coach Standard

- Share your story and why you care;

- Define non-negotiables and team values.

3. Call parents or guardians personally

- Introduce yourself and express that you're building men, not just athletes;

- Ask them, "Is there anything I should know to better support your son?"

4. Start a notebook for documenting leadership moments, challenges, and observations

Phase 2: Days 11 through 20 – Set the Standard & Enforce It

Priorities:

- Start layering in discipline, accountability, and structure;

- Make expectations visible and enforceable.

Action Steps:

1. Implement the Warrior Coach Weekly Blueprint *(See Toolbox Chapter)*

- Leadership talks, culture checks, cadence drills.

2. Create "buy-in moments" through adversity

- Run a tough practice or workout and celebrate those who respond well.

3. Identify and empower your first Culture Captains

- Ask, "Who's stepping up without being told?"

4. Set up your Standard Bearer system

- Weekly recognition for the player who embodies team values.

5. Address your first discipline issue firmly but fairly

- Use it as a teaching moment for the team.

Phase 3: Days 21 through 30 – Build Momentum & Brotherhood
Priorities:

- Shift from compliance to commitment;

- Build unity through shared struggle and ownership.

Action Steps:

1. Host your first team event

- Ideas: Team cookout, community-service project, leadership retreat;

- Purpose: deepen connection and team identity.

2. Introduce player-led components

- Captains lead warmups or drills;

- Peer-to-peer accountability moments: "Who do we need to encourage or challenge today?"

3. Create a leadership board or wall in locker room

- Post values, quotes, player goals, Standard Bearers.

4. Start collecting stories

- Ask players to write or share what the team means to them so far.

5. Finish with a State-of-the-Team Talk

- Recap wins, lessons, and what's next;

- Reinforce that "this is just the beginning—our mission starts now."

Tips for New Warrior Coaches

- **Be consistent.** Your presence and energy must match your message.

- **Celebrate small wins.** Early momentum matters.

- **Overcommunicate with parents and staff.** Alignment is leadership.

- **Don't wait to lead.** Every day is a culture moment.

- **Document everything.** Track progress, patterns, and breakthroughs.

Final Word

Your players won't remember every drill or speech from these first 30 days.

But they will remember if you made them feel seen, challenged, and believed in.

They'll remember if you showed up with clarity and conviction, or if you just blew the whistle and hoped for the best.

This first month is your foundation.

Build it strong. Lead it well. Set the tone now—and the culture will carry itself later.

Chapter 15

Answering the Call: The Mission Continues

Now it's your turn. The torch has been passed. Step forward, lead boldly, and become the coach they'll never forget.

If you've made it this far, it means something in this book has stirred you. Something in you knows it's time to lead.

You might be a coach already. Or a dad. A teacher. A veteran. Or just a man ready to lead.

Good. Because the world needs you.

Step In. Lead Boldly.

Young men everywhere are struggling—not just on the field, but in figuring out who they are, where they're going, and how to keep getting back up when life knocks them down.

And you don't need to have it all figured out. You just need to be willing to step up, get in the fight, and lead with purpose.

This is your invitation.

Start where you are. Coach a youth team. Volunteer at a school. Mentor one kid. Or just lead your own family better.

You don't need credentials or a title—just the courage to start. What matters most? Heart. And the courage to use it.

And when you lead with steady hands, a strong heart, and unshakable commitment, everything changes.

The world doesn't just need more coaches.

It needs more Warrior Coaches.

Lace up. Find your field. And become the man they'll never forget.

Time to step in. Time to lead.

Warrior Coach Toolkit

Expectations for Coaches – Sample

1. Be loyal to the head coach, the players, and the community;

2. **The following is expected from all coaches in our program:**

3. Always act with integrity;

4. Provide quality training and leadership to our athletes;

5. Have a passion for coaching and not just be a clock-puncher;

6. Assist our athletes on and off the field, even after they graduate;

7. Treat our players as young men, and show them love and respect;

8. Make decisions based solely on what's best for the team;

9. Make our school the best place to get an education and play football;

10. Help develop young men into good sons, fathers, husbands, and members of their community.

Coach to Parent First Call – Sample

"Hi Mr./Mrs. ___, I'm Coach ___ and I just wanted to introduce myself. I want to let you know that your son is a part of something special. In our program we're not just building football players—we're shaping future husbands, fathers, and leaders in society. If there's anything going on at home you'd want me to know so I can better support him, I'm all ears. Please reach out to me if anything goes on in the future that you think I should know. We're in this together. Welcome to the (program name) family."

Daily Team Meeting Agenda – Sample

1. **Quick Wins**: Share player highlights from practice, game, or life.

2. **Leadership Lesson:** Brief message from coach (<5 mins).

3. **Player Shout-outs**: Teammates recognize each other.

4. **Review of Team Standard**: Remind them what we stand for.

5. **Focus for Today**: One mission point (e.g., toughness, unity, discipline).

6. **Share the Plan for the Day**: Give brief verbal overview of plan to players and a detailed physical copy to all coaches

Player & Parent Welcome Letter – Sample

Head Coach Your Name

   Cell Phone: (XXX)XXX-XXXX

   E-Mail: example@school.com

To all 9th-12th grade football players & parents:

Welcome to a new year of football. This year looks to have plenty of excitement and in-county action! **The first day of practice will be Monday, August 11, from 6:00 p.m. until 8:00 p.m. If you have any questions, please text or call.**

Representing Our School

We, as a community, must represent the school in a positive way. As coaches, players, and parents, we must always encourage each other to refrain from negative behavior. Football is not a perfect game. The kids will make mistakes, I will make mistakes, and the officials will make mistakes. It is important to always learn from these mistakes and look to the future in a positive light, encouraging your athlete to do the best they can. If any problems should come up, please talk to me as soon as possible. Communication is the key to a successful program.

Playing Time

Playing time is determined by performance at practice, attitude, and the skill level of the athlete. **Playing time is not equal for every athlete.** It is my intention to try to provide a positive experience for every athlete on the team. As a coach, I will try my hardest to play your athlete as much as possible while still being competitive in different game situations. With this being the case, your athlete may experience different amounts of playing time from game to game and situation to situation.

Family & School Situations If your child must miss practice or games, let me know as soon as possible. I will try to accommodate your athlete and your situation to meet his or her needs to the best of my ability. Please understand that these decisions will be on a case-by-case basis and require appropriate advanced notice.

Accountability & Consequences

It is important for your student-athlete to understand that being part of a team is a privilege. They are not only representing themselves through their actions, but also their parents, teammates, coaches, athletic director, school, and the community. Your athlete must be academically eligible to participate in games, and we will follow the school's eligibility policy. The following will be used throughout the year as a course of action in case your son abuses the privilege of organized athletics.

Infractions

Late or absent from practice. The head coach will have the discretion as to how the player will make up the conditioning and practice that was missed. This will also impact whether he starts and/or his playing time.

Late or absent for game. First time: warning; second time: one-game suspension; third time: suspension for remainder of season .

*Exceptions **MAY** be considered with appropriate advanced notice from parents*

Communication

I have an open-door policy and invite positive parental feedback and involvement in our program. If you have concerns, please wait 24 hours before making contact to allow adrenaline and emotion to be minimized for all involved. If you would like to meet about a situation that occurred, please let me know. All issues should be handled in the following order: (1) Player talks to coach; (2) Player and parents talk to coach; (3) Athletic director gets involved only if necessary and after these steps have been followed.

Finally, I hope we can all work together as a team to make this season fun and exciting. I hope to instill respect, responsibility, and a strong work ethic that your athletes can use for the rest of their lives.

Sincerely,

Your Name

Varsity Football Coach

Weekly Leadership Blueprint – Sample

Monday: *Set the Tone*

- Team talk on mindset or leadership theme (10 min)

- Positional coach check-ins: Ask your assistants who needs encouragement or accountability.

- Film review and self-evaluation

Tuesday: *Toughness Tuesday*

- Create adversity: challenge-based drill or scenario

- Emphasize composure under fire: "How we handle pressure is who we are."

- Hardest conditioning day of the week

Wednesday: *Situational Awareness*

- Mental reps: walk-through, opposing team scout, team strategy discussions

- Player-led feedback sessions: "What do we need to clean up?"

Thursday: *Culture Check/Mission Ready*

- Walk-through and mental visualization

- Positional coach check-ins: "How did we embody our theme of the week?"

- End practice by recognizing leadership moments from the week

Weekly Practice Plan Template – Sample

Monday: Mental-Toughness Monday

- Brief leadership lesson or story

- Conditioning-heavy day

- Competitive team period to finish

Tuesday: Technique Tuesday

- Position drills

- Install new plays or concepts

- Individual competition periods

Wednesday: Situational Wednesday

- Team Drills

- Red zone

- 2-minute drill

- Goal-line and 4th down situations

Thursday: Walk through & Details

- Special teams focus

- Scripted walk through

- Team stretches and mindset prep

- End with team dinner

Friday: Game day

- Final gear checks

- Quick team check-in

- Energy, focus, and discipline reminders

5 Core Coaching Tools

1. The One-Minute One-on-One

- Ask, "How's school? How's home? How can I help?"

- Listen without interrupting.

- Offer a clear challenge or encouragement.

- Follow up in a week or two.

2. Warrior Cadence Drill *(See Chapter 3)*

- Use in emotional fire training or end-of-practice conditioning.

- Builds focus under fatigue.

3. Gear-Check Protocol *(See Chapter 6)*

- Simple system before road games: accountability and discipline.

- Use team leaders to run the process.

4. Standard-Bearer Award

- Celebrate at team dinner or meeting.

- Rotate categories: Integrity, Toughness, Leadership, etc.

5. Culture Captains

- Weekly recognition for the player who best lives out the Warrior

Values.

- Select two or three players to monitor energy, effort, and team behavior

- Give them permission to speak up and hold teammates accountable

- This is an opportunity to give recognition in addition to your normal captains

Templates – Copy and Use

Weekly Leadership Traits Tracker – Coach Use

Use a 1–5 scale and track weekly to monitor growth.

- Integrity [ ]

- Toughness [ ]

- Consistency [ ]

- Attitude [ ]

- Coachability [ ]

Start-of-Season "My Mission Plan" – Player Self-Evaluation

- What are my three goals this season?

- What habits am I committing to daily?

- How will I respond when things get tough?

- Who am I accountable to?

End-of-Season Player Evaluation Form

- **Discipline**: [ ] Consistent [ ] Inconsistent [ ] Needs Work

- **Effort Level**: [ ] All-Out [ ] Moderate [ ] Passive

- **Coachability**: [ ] High [ ] Average [ ] Struggles

- **Team Contribution**: [ ] Leader [ ] Role Player [ ] Disruptive

Leave space for written feedback and set goals for next season.

Player-Correction Script

Sometimes, players mess up. Here's a quick three-step framework:
1. **Stop and make eye contact;**

2. **Correct with clarity.** Example: "You're better than that. You owe your focus to the team on every snap";

3. **End with belief.** "Get back in there. You've got this. Show me."

What to do when:
A player breaks down emotionally:
Pull them aside. Ask, "What's going on in your life?" Listen first, coach second.

A parent challenges your authority:
Stay calm. Say, "Let's talk about this later. I'm here to coach your son, not argue."

A player quits:
Meet with them one-on-one. "What's leading you to this decision?" Leave the door open but protect team culture.

Final Word

You don't rise to the occasion, you fall to the level of your training. That's why tools like these matter.

These aren't just checklists, they're commitments. They help you lead with purpose, consistency, and a warrior's mindset.

Use them. Modify them. Make them your own. But most of all—*live them.*

Your team will follow the systems you enforce, not the words you say.

Train with clarity. Lead with purpose. And watch your culture become unbreakable.

Call to Action

If you were impacted by a Warrior Coach—or if you've become one yourself—we want to hear your story.

- When did a Warrior Coach make a difference in your life?

- What moment do you still carry with you?

- What lessons stuck with you beyond the field?

Submit your testimonial to be included in the extended edition of this book or future Warrior Coach resources.

Email: contact@The-Warrior-Coach.com

Let's build this legacy—together.

What do others have to say?

From Dustin N.

"I got my first coaching job under Coach Sedelmaier, and I couldn't have asked for a better mentor to give me a start. The players were respectful, well-mannered, and disciplined. I was very impressed with my time on the staff, because there is a ton of love in that program. Even though I was not a part of the community, I was still treated like family from the start. I really miss being a part of it."

From Taylor B.

"Inside my closet, I have a t-shirt from when I was a toddler. On the front it says, "Future OHS Portager," on the back there is a signature from "*Justin Sedelmaier #32.*" Little did he, or I know, that this high school kid would be one of my high school football coaches at that same school.

Thinking back on some of my most memorable moments from my football career, I can picture Coach Sedelmaier going crazy on the sideline. Coach was always the first to celebrate a big play. Jumping up and down, screaming, and big fist pumps; these aren't just emotions of big plays for him, this is the intensity he coached with. It wasn't just out of his love for the game of football, but also from his love and care for all of his players.

Brotherhood and teamwork, were the two biggest things I learned from Coach Sedelmaier. We all knew about his military background; he was proud of it, and shared it with us. This structure and leadership he brought to our team because of it, helped us grow and work together better than ever. I vividly remember Coach running out on the field and picking up players over his shoulders that were cramping, and running them off the field. He always did what was best for the team and it was actions like this, along with the faith he had in the brotherhood, created lifelong lessons for everyone.

Coach Sedelmaier is a hell of a coach and a hell of a man! I am proud to have been one of his players and I wish him nothing but success in his future!"

About the Author

Justin Sedelmaier is a United States Marine Corps combat veteran and high school head football coach who has spent his life leading warriors—from Afghanistan to the American football sideline.

After leaving the military and struggling to find purpose in civilian life, Justin rediscovered his mission through mentoring young men. Today, he coaches not just for wins, but to shape players into future husbands, fathers, and leaders.

Through The Warrior Coach, Justi n shares his no-nonsense approach to leadership that is rooted in discipline, consistency, and care. His work empowers coaches, dads, and veterans to lead with clarity, confidence, and heart.

He lives with his family in the Midwest and continues to speak, coach, and serve through his growing Warrior Coach platform.

Visit the website: https://the-warrior-coach.com

Join the newsletter: https://the-warrior-coach.kit.com/2205a92e30